First Picture Dictionary
Animals
첫 번째 그림 사전
동물

Butterfly
나비

Pig
돼지

Fox
여우

Rabbit
토끼

Illustrated by Anna Ivanir

www.kidkiddos.com
Copyright ©2025 by KidKiddos Books Ltd.
support@kidkiddos.com

All rights reserved. No part of this book may be reproduced in any form or by any electronic or mechanical means, including information storage and retrieval systems, without written permission from the publisher, except in the case of a reviewer, who may quote brief passages embodied in critical articles or in a review.
First edition, 2025

Library and Archives Canada Cataloguing in Publication
First Picture Dictionary - Animals (English Korean Bilingual edition)
ISBN: 978-1-83416-594-3 paperback
ISBN: 978-1-83416-595-0 hardcover
ISBN: 978-1-83416-593-6 eBook

Wild Animals
야생 동물

Hippopotamus
하마

Panda
판다

Fox
여우

Rhino
코뿔소

Deer
사슴

Moose
무스

Wolf
늑대

✦ *A moose is a great swimmer and can dive underwater to eat plants!*

✦ 무스는 수영을 잘하고 물속에 잠수해 식물을 먹을 수 있어요!

Squirrel
다람쥐

Koala
코알라

✦ *A squirrel hides nuts for winter, but sometimes forgets where it put them!*

✦ 다람쥐는 겨울을 위해 견과류를 숨기지만, 가끔 어디에 뒀는지 잊어버려요!

Gorilla
고릴라

Pets
반려동물

Canary
카나리아

Guinea Pig
기니피그

✦ *A frog can breathe through its skin as well as its lungs!*
✦ 개구리는 폐뿐만 아니라 피부로도 숨을 쉴 수 있어요!

Frog
개구리

Hamster
햄스터

Goldfish
금붕어

Dog
개

> ✦*Some parrots can copy words and even laugh like a human!*
> ✦어떤 앵무새는 말을 따라 하고 사람처럼 웃기도 해요!

Cat
고양이

Parrot
앵무새

Mosquito
모기

Dragonfly
잠자리

✦A dragonfly was one of the first insects on Earth, even before dinosaurs!
✦잠자리는 지구에 나타난 가장 오래된 곤충 중 하나로 공룡보다도 먼저 있었어요!

Bee
벌

Butterfly
나비

Ladybug
무당벌레

Small Animals
작은 동물

Chameleon
카멜레온

Spider
거미

✦ *An ostrich is the biggest bird, but it cannot fly!*
✦ 타조는 가장 큰 새지만, 날 수는 없어요!

Bee
벌

✦ *A snail carries its home on its back and moves very slowly.*
✦ 달팽이는 등에 집을 이고, 아주 천천히 움직여요.

Snail
달팽이

Mouse
생쥐

Quiet Animals
조용한 동물

Ladybug
무당벌레

Turtle
거북이

✦ *A turtle can live both on land and in water.*
✦ 거북이는 육지와 물속 모두에서 살 수 있어요.

Fish
물고기

Lizard
도마뱀

Nighttime Animals
야행성 동물

Firefly
반딧불이

Badger
오소리

Kiwi Bird
키위새

Leopard
표범

Hedgehog
고슴도치

Owl
부엉이

Bat
박쥐

◆An owl hunts at night and uses its hearing to find food!
◆부엉이는 밤에 사냥하며 청각으로 먹이를 찾아요!

◆A firefly glows at night to find other fireflies.
◆반딧불이는 밤에 빛을 내어 다른 반딧불이를 찾아요.

Raccoon
너구리

Tarantula
타란튤라

Colorful Animals
다채로운 동물

A flamingo is pink
플라밍고는 분홍색이에요

An owl is brown
부엉이는 갈색이에요

A swan is white
백조는 하얀색이에요

An octopus is purple
문어는 보라색이에요

A frog is green
개구리는 초록색이에요

✦ *A frog is green, so it can hide among the leaves.*
✦ 개구리는 초록색이기 때문에 잎 사이에 숨을 수 있어요.

Animals and Their Babies
동물과 새끼들

Cow and Calf
소와 송아지

Cat and Kitten
고양이와 새끼 고양이

✦ *A chick talks to its mother even before it hatches.*
✦ 병아리는 알에서 태어나기 전에도 엄마와 대화해요.

Chicken and Chick
닭과 병아리

Dog and Puppy
개와 강아지

Butterfly and Caterpillar
나비와 애벌레

Sheep and Lamb
양과 새끼양

Horse and Foal
말과 망아지

Pig and Piglet
돼지와 새끼 돼지

Goat and Kid
염소와 새끼 염소

www.ingramcontent.com/pod-product-compliance
Lightning Source LLC
LaVergne TN
LVHW072002060526
838200LV00010B/264